1

Ash Wednesday

Elham Khalil

©   Elham Khalil, 2011
ISBN   978-94-90615-02-4

Elhamkhalil3@gmail.com
www.elhamkhalil.com
www.copticmuseum.com

Cover
Illustration by Claartje van der Linden

Elham Khalil was born in 1947 in Egypt,
lives since 1970 in the Netherlands,
studied at Cairo, Amsterdam and Oxford
Universities, has Doctoral Anglo-Irish
Drama and PhD Social Sciences and
International Communication, has long
media career in Dutch broadcasting, and
35 years experience of management of the
family farm in Dutch Veluwe countryside.
Elham Khalil established and ran the
Coptic Museum in Ruinerwold,
Netherlands beween 1999 and 2006. Now
it is on www.compitcmuseumonline.com
Her love for stage started in her teens,
besides plays and screen scenario she
writes on the Coptic Church and culture.

Also by Elham Khalil

Plays
Somebody's Aunt, Stealing The Sea
Ash Wednesday, The Foyer Bell
Wrinkles, The Missing Member
One Free Ticket, Smell In My Brain
Loosing My Face, The Womb
Coma Beach, Adoption Plan
Till Death Do Us Part
Historic Plays
Coptos

Short stories
Children Of The Mind
The Coin
The Third Child

Christian writings
I.Nspriation
My Bible
Sayings
De Eerste Kinderjaren van Jezus
De Heilige Familie in Egypte (Dutch Etition)
Early Childhood of Jesus in Egypt
The Holy Family in Egypt
De Koptische Kerk: Vraag en Antwoord (Dutch)
"The Coptic Church: Question And Answer"

Characters

Mathew a priest, end thirties
Luke his brother, begin thirties,
environment and animal activist
Boyd their father, begin seventies, land
developer
Julie Luke's' wife, end twenties
Tom tower and church take-carer. Old.
Deaf.
Seven choir boys and girls
Dara's voice, Boyd dead wife

The children

May thirteen
Elizabeth nine
Annemarie seven
Martin fourteen
Kevin fifteen
Matt twelve
Joe eight

Time the 1990s
Place England

Ash Wednesday was first read to my daughters, Sendy and Maria, on Christmas Day, Monday 25 December 2007, Bristol, UK

Act one
Scene One
Tuesday Morning

Complete darkness.
The sound of swift movements of bats, church bell and wind in tree leafs.
Silence.
Morning light.
The green surrounding the church, the tower and the yew.
Upstage centre is the tower door leading to the partly seen cylinder staircase. Far right is the church door, far left is the yew with three trunks of which one is partly hollow with a man-tall grove, and one is leafless, lying almost horizontal. Three or four old park benches scattered around the tree. The narrow path leading to the church and the graveyard is far left and upstage left.
Children's voices laughing and talking draw nearer.
Children enter carrying happy birthday decorations, congratulation signs, ribbons and balloons. They start putting them between the church, the tower and the yew.

May   You forgot it again Martin.

Martin   What?

May   The ladder.

Martin   I didn't. Tom needs it.

May   To do what?
Martin   I don't know.

10

Elizabeth He's fixing the bell.

Matt Again?

The tower bell rings, loud, everybody covers his ears.
Silence.

Joe Are we going to hear it by night?

Elizabeth Sure, when bats…

Matt Stop it Liz. Don't worry Joe. Come. Let's finish it.

They start fixing decorations.

Annemarie Come on Liz! On Martin's shoulders?

Elizabeth I can't do that!

Matt I'll do it.

Kevin We should've waited till tomorrow. It wouldn't survive night attacks.

Elizabeth Dinnertime!

Martin Would you stop bothering about bats Kevin? Father Mathew wants it ready today.
Joe Who's having dinner by night?
Matt You know Joe.

Annemarie   You know Joe. Bats.

Joe   Can I do this one?

Kevin   Here you go.

He carries him on his shoulders.

May   Kevin is right, if we want visitors to see any of this.

Matt   Everybody will see it.

Elizabeth   Covered with droppings?

Martin   Would you stop it now Liz? We still have twenty balloons to blow.

Annemarie   Balloons?

Joe   Balloons!

The girls start blowing balloons with small balloon-blowers, while boys fix the decorations. Matt on Martin's shoulders, Joe on Kevin's shoulders, shaking, girls laugh at the sight. Jo and Annemarie start taking some mud and put on each other's forehead some black crosses, teasing each other and laughing. Tom, with headphones is seen descending the last few steps of the tower. They grab the ladder. He starts turning the bell handle, inside the tower door. Kevin sees Tom doing that, and looks up.
Kevin   The bell, the bell!

They all cover their ears while Tom turns the electric bell. Silence. Bell does not go off. They relax, apprehensive. Tom smiles knowing they were expecting to hear the bell.
Everybody in the play talks to Tom in words as in sign language. Tom speaks, but one can hear he is deaf.

May   You're lucky Tom. It doesn't bother you a bit, does it?

Tom smiles.

May   How do you know if it's working?

Tom   I know.

Kevin   What do you need this for Tom? You can't hear the bats.

Tom   I told you, council people gave it to me to listen.

Joe and Annemarie laugh silently.

Matt   But it's for detecting bats and sealing up their places.

Tom   *Irritated*   And I sealed all places Matt. Didn't I?

Martin   You're right Tom, for months you did nothing else.
Elizabeth   *To Martin*   How did he do it?

Annemarie   Yes, how did you do it Tom?

Martin   Annemarie?

Tom   If you keep quiet, you can listen to everything Annemarie, also bats.

Annemarie   *She closes her eyes and keeps silent*   Can you hear me now?

Tom   I hear you Annemarie. You want to blow balloons.

Annemarie is surprised. Eyes wide open.
They laugh.

Kevin   Nobody is allowed to go up.

Annemarie   My father is going up tomorrow. You can come with us Kevin.

Kevin   Everybody is allowed to go up tomorrow.

Joe   I'll come with you.

Kevin   We can take some balloons with us.

May   I still don't understand why they needed to open this old tower now?

Martin   It belongs to the church.

Matt I don't think so. Father Mathew said it was built for war, and it looks much older than anything else.

Tom Wrong.

May What's wrong Tom?

Tom tries to reach for something in a grove of the tree, partly disappears, he looks from the grove, talks and then disappears.

Tom The yew came first.

He disappears then his head appears.

More than one thousand year later came the tower.

He disappears, comes back.

Hundreds of years later came the church.

He disappears.
Silence.

Joe And when are you coming back Tom?
Annemarie He is gone! Tom!

Elizabeth Don't do that. He doesn't hear you.

Martin He hears the bats.

Kevin And the bell.

Tom comes back with an old book. They tease him by trying to get the book and headphones.

Matt The book! Anything you ask him, he grabs his old book.

Martin What kind of book is it?

Kevin So the tree stood alone for many years Tom?

Tom The tree was never alone Kevin. There was always a crowd around here. There was no tower or army and there was no church or prayers, but everybody came here to pray.

May Pray for what if there was no church?

Tom Pray for the whole world. They came to understand the world, and talk about themselves, share their feelings and pain and they wanted to be cured.

Joe Were they all sick?
Tom No. They came to celebrate the New Year.

May What new year?

Tom The new year of the earth.

Tom sits on one of the benches and begins to turn the pages as if looking for something, making sure nobody would snatch the book.

Kevin What did they want to understand?

Tom continues looking at his book.
Elizabeth leans on Tom, looking.

Elizabeth It's a Bible.

May *Leaning* Not the one we have in church.

Kevin He has two bibles, one for praying and one for answering questions.

Annemarie snatches the book, gives it to Elizabeth, Tom grabs it back, continues looking in it.

Matt He showed it to me once.

Joe He did?

Joe snatches the book, looks in its pages. They form a kind of circle that Tom can't reach to his book, Matt leans over.
Joe It's full of strange names.

Annemarie Drawings.

Elizabeth Trees.

May Plants and animals.

Martin And it's written in red.

Kevin Red? *Leans over Martin*

Matt By hand.

Joe Bloody hands?

Annemarie Of bats!

Joe You frighten me Annemarie.

Matt "See all these bats, they do us many favours"
Laughs Nonsense!

Kevin *Takes it and looks in some pages* "The yew, is the oldest tree, it can live thousands of years and can live forever." Spooky business!

Joe Hoooooo!

Annemarie You frighten me Joe.

In the meantime Tom gives up and busies himself with cutting small branches from the yew.

Kevin Who wrote it?

Martin It's a dodgy book. If bats are doing us favours and the yew can live forever, I am king Arthur!

Pretending to be a king with some decorative piece, tree branch and balloon.
Mathew enters. He is a Catholic priest.
They all feel embarrassed, give the book to Tom.

18

Father Mathew   Leave Tom alone. It's our last rehearsing day. Remember?

Elizabeth   I was hoping it was yesterday.

Father Mathew   Tomorrow as you all know is the opening of the tower, and everybody will be listening to your singing.

Kevin   I want to read Tom's bible father.

Father Mathew   Tom's bible?

Kevin   Tom's book.

Father Mathew   I'm afraid it's up to Tom to decide. Off you go now. Martin you are in charge.

Elizabeth   Can't we sing here? I hate going in there.

Annemarie   I feel sick.

Matt   And I can't concentrate; they are watching us.

Father Mathew   Don't pay attention Matt.

Martin   They pay us attention father.

Father Mathew   We can't bring the piano outside. Annemarie, the hats?

Annemarie takes some small white Chinese type of hats out of a paper bag.

Annemarie   Aunty Rose says it is a present.

Father Mathew   You shouldn't forget to thank aunt Rose Annemarie.

They start putting them on.

Matt   We'll be singing in Chinese now.

He starts some Chinese notes.

Kevin   And we look stupid.

Martin   We'll look more stupid with the droppings.

Anne   Everybody will be laughing.

Tom starts to laugh. Joe and Annemarie join him. Father Mathew looks at them, they stop.

Father Mathew   You look magnificent. Off you go and keep them on.

Children go to church.
Tom looks at some pages in his book, pleased.

Father Mathew   You should find another place for keeping them Tom.

Tom   She said it's the best place.

Father Mathew   Seven years now since she gave it to you. She trusted nobody else with what she was writing.

Tom   I have to know what would happen if we cut big branches. I know she did mention something about it.

Father Mathew   You cut branches every year Tom.

Tom   I only cut small ones for decorating the church on Palm Sunday and burn them to use one year later on Ash Wednesday. This is different. You want to cut big branches to widen the entrance. I don't like it. Dara wouldn't have liked it either.

Father Mathew   Mother wouldn't have liked to cut anything. Now that you mention it, where is the ash?

Tom   I box is beside the altar together with the blessed water and incense.

Father Mathew   *Sitting facing the tower and the church* All these years...

Tom   They thought she was...

Father Mathew   I know what they thought, nobody knew what she was doing. She wrote even on bats.

Standing, looking up.

But you did seal the tower.

Tom   They're gone from up there, to in here.

Choir singing.

Are we going to seal the church after Easter?

Father Mathew   Only if we can secure some financial support Tom.

Tom   I know. It's costly and no one would give money for such a thing.

Father Mathew   God will provide.
Tom   She loved the tree and the tower.

Father Mathew   And the church Tom?

Tom   And the church.

Sits, reading.

Father Mathew   You better hurry with clearing the entrance.

Tom goes to the narrow passage between the tree and the entrance of the tower and spreads his arms.

Tom   Isn't this big enough?

Father Mathew   It's more than enough for us, but we have to consider visitors now. And brides and bridegrooms can hardly walk through. Bride dresses, remember?

Tom   Two tails and one veil!

Father Mathew   You counted them!

Tom   *Laughing* And the fat one?

Father Mathew   The bell is doing fine. For now, it's meant only for Sundays.

Tom looks up, and Father Mathew does the same.

Father Mathew   She used to say one day we'll see the yew from the top of the tower.
Tom   She sees it now.

Act One
Scene Two
In Church

The song ends and the lights come up from three chandeliers showing the arched ceiling with its wooden panes where bats hang in groups. The altar and some benches are covered with old filthy cheats of table cloths, bed sheets and plastic spreads, stained with yellow, brown and black bat droppings. Choir area and piano are clean. Sporadically bats move swiftly from one corner to the other, with a specific sudden windy noise. They affect the lights and candles, dropping on children, books and benches.
Children start taking the rest of the covers from a corner and spread them on the uncovered altar and benches in disgust, but with care. Couple of them start collecting choir books and place them on one of the benches and cover them.

Martin   How come that every thing is covered with droppings except Tom's book?

Matt   He keeps it in the tree.

Kevin   That's even worse; bats are numerous in there.

May   That's true, now that the tower is cleared.

Annemarie   I know why. Bats keep their home clean and drop only outside.

Elizabeth   Like cats!

24

Kevin There must be a reason.

Father Mathew comes in.

Annemarie Why is it that Tom's book is not covered with droppings Father?

Father Mathew He keeps it in the tree.

Matt I told you.

Martin May be we should ask the bats.

Kevin He said people used to come and ask for knowledge.

May I'll clean up the altar.

Father Mathew You did that yesterday. It's Martins' turn. You do the benches.

May And the books?

Father Mathew It's Kevin's turn. Who is taking care of the candles?

Annemarie Nobody.

Father Mathew Nobody?

Joe They are all clean.

Matt You mean they're all burnt.

Joe   I kept them burning yesterday. Mother says bats hate candles.

Father Mathew   Promise me you wouldn't do such a thing again Joe. And now fetch me the ash box?

Joe brings a box

Father Mathew   Put it carefully on the altar.

Annemarie   Can I help you father?

Father Mathew   Of course Annemarie. Tell me, what day is it tomorrow?

Annemarie   Ash Wednesday.

Father Mathew   Thank you. Martin fetch me the bag.

Martin brings an old bag, Father Mathew takes a flacon filled with water and places it beside the box.

Father Mathew   Now you can cover it.

Elizabeth   Why do you put water on the ash father?

Father Mathew   To bless the ash, and the cross we make on the forehead stays for a while.

Annemarie   Who said we should do that?

Father Mathew   Nobody in particular, but long ago…

Joe   Before the tree?

Father Mathew   May be not that long, but long ago people did that to repent.

Annemarie   What is to repent?

Father Mathew   To feel bad about something one has done, and would never like to do again.

Annemarie   *Thinks, comes forward in a serious manner* I like to repent father.

They laugh.

Father Mathew   Repent what Annemarie?

Annemarie   *Solemnly*   I feel very bad about cleaning up the mess of the bats everyday, and I don't want to do that ever again.

They all laugh.

Matt   Very clever!

Father Mathew   Last year we said something about Ash Wednesday, can anybody tell me why we celebrate it tomorrow, and not last month or next month?

May It's forty-six days before Easter, when we start Lent fasting.

Father Mathew That's right May.

Joe But why ash?

Father Mathew Any one can answer Joe?

Martin You said last year at the beginning of mass "Remember man that you are dust and to dust you will return". To remind every one that people become dust when they die.

Father Mathew Excellent Martin. Annemarie, can you remind me tomorrow of what May and Martin have just said?

Annemarie You keep on forgetting father. You should write it down.

Father Mathew I know, that's why I need you Annemarie. And now, all of you should concentrate on tomorrow.

Martin Not on the droppings, and where they would hit next.
May You should've seen the face of my mother last week putting my clothes in the washing machine.

Martin My mother doesn't mind. She loves the ugly beasts.

28

Elizabeth   And she doesn't come to church.

Father Mathew   Bats are no reason for not coming to church.

Kevin   But how can we protect ourselves?

Father Mathew   Bats are protected from people Kevin, and people have to protect themselves. At least we have clean heads today.

Joe   Poor baldhead of my uncle!

Kevin   It's easier to clean than yours!

Martin   They love hair!

Elizabeth   *To Joe* Yours in particular!

May   We should give hats to everybody coming to church.

Martin   It would cost a fortune.

Father Mathew   Children we have to start.
Elizabeth   How long do we have to keep on cleaning?

Father Mathew   As long as they are up there.

Looking up.

Joe   Don't!

Annemarie gives Father Mathew a hat. He keeps it in hand.

Father Mathew   Thank you.

Kevin   They used to drive bats by burning incense, isn't that right father?

May   How do you know that?

Kevin   Tom told me.

Father Mathew   In the Middle Ages people drove bats and evil spirits and lots of other things with incense.

Martin   May be that's what Tom was doing all these months up there. Clearing bats with incense.

Kevin   If he can hear bats with his detectors, he'd drive them mad with incense.

Matt   I was picking worms under the tree…
Annemarie   To eat?

Matt   No! Tom asked me to leave them alone for they're night meal for bats.

Annemarie   Good for them.

Matt   For bats?

Annemarie   No, for worms.

Father Mathew   We pray all bats would be gone before long.

Martin   Naphthalene crystals didn't work father.

May   Floods of lights didn't either.

Father Mathew   Drafts my children, drafts. We hope we can order fans, big fans to do the job. But tomorrow the tower opens its doors, and it is Ash Wednesday, come, let us sing!

Act one
Scene Three
Early Evening
Near The Tree

The tower bell is lighted and beams misty light on the yew tree. Far right the church is lighted with couple of candles. The choir sings one of the evening songs. One can only see silhouettes with songbooks in hand, Tom comes in and sits outside on one of the benches, looks at the yew tree, arranges some material for cutting hedges, moving some branches, separating small and big ones. His book is on one of the benches. Mark comes in on a motorbike, wearing jeans and t-shirt, with a Save the Bats logo. Julie is on the seat behind. She is pregnant. He has a white long roll in one of his hands. Tom does not notice Mark who puts the loud engine off. Mark touches Tom's shoulder, and Tom turns and gives a sign of surprise, recognition and welcoming.

Mark   How are you Tom?

Tom   Mark! I can't believe it!

Mark   Nice to see you again Tom.

Tom   Mark! Five years my boy!

He makes the number five with his hand.

Mark   Yes five years.

Tom   Why?
Mark   Why did I leave?

Tom Yes.

Mark shows his chest with Save the Bats logo.

Mark It doesn't matter, that's why I come back!

Mark and Julie show their t-shirts with the same logo.

Tom, this is Julie, my wife. Julie, this is Tom. Without him nothing will be done around here.

Julie Hi Tom.

Tom smiles and nods.

Mark No Julie. Try your hands as well.

Julie *Putting two hands on her chest* I am Julie *and on her belly* and these is my babies!

Tom tries to understand, stretches his hand almost touching her big belly, lifting two fingers.

Julie Yes! *Lifting two fingers*

Mark It used to be dark here.

Tom *Touching Mark t-shirt* They're all in the tree now.
Mark looks upset.

Mark It was exciting playing in the dark. Remember? Touching darkness?

33

Pause.

Come Julie, we have to find my brother.

Mark sees the book, lifts it and looks at it as if thinking of a distant memory. Some bats fly from the tree to the tower and back again. Puts the book on the bench.

Mark Listen.

Tom *Laughing* I'm listening my whole life Mark, and never heard a thing.

Mark Listen Julie, their eco location, that's how they find their way in the dark.

Julie listening. Tom takes headphones off and puts it on her ears. Julie listens excited with what she hears.

Mark Who gave you this Tom?

Tom Council people.

Julie To find the bats?

Tom And seal their nests.

Mark Where is Mathew? I have to talk to him about the tower.

Tom It's the tree I'm worried about.

34

Mark   The tree will be standing right here for another thousand years. Don't worry Tom.

Bats fly swiftly between the tower and the tree, Mark looks tenderly.

Aren't they beautiful?

Tom shakes his head in disbelief. Mark goes to the church. Julie lingers behind, giving him back the headphones, looking at the tower, then being attracted to the tree, playfully going around it, with her hands touching its leaves. Sits on the horizontal trunk, touches it. Tom is eyeing her with concerned surprise. She looks into the grove.

Julie   It's a strange tree Tom.

He does not answer. As she is about to pick one little leave, he hurries to her and prevents her in annoyed mumbling. She looks at him in surprise and fear, hurries after Mark.

Act one
Scene Four
Same Evening
In Church

Mark and Julie stand at the entrance of the church. Father Mathew is blowing off one of the candles.

Father Mathew I'm coming Tom.

Mark Tom is still outside.

Father Mathew turns in surprise, hesitates for a moment, he sees Julie, steps forward and shakes hands.

Father Mathew Mark, what a surprise!

Mark Here is another surprise, Julie, my wife, Mathew, my brother.

Julie Nice to meet you. Mark told me you're a priest of many beliefs.

Father Mathew I wasn't aware of that.

Julie But I never knew what you mean darling?

Mark Mathew was devoted to nature, like our dear mother, but when father disappeared he thought of joining Church of England, and when mother died he changed it for Rome.

Julie   Oh, it sounds evolutionary. You take over disappearing after your father darling. But why did he disappear?

Father Mathew   Mark would know the answer. He went after him.

Julie looks around trying to find somewhere clean to sit. Father Mathew removes one cover of one of the benches. She sits, uncomfortably. Mark sits on one of the covered benches.

Julie   Nice place to live in.

Father Mathew   I don't live here.

Julie   I meant the bats.

Father Mathew   The bats? Yes, unfortunately they do live here.

Mark   Big day tomorrow?

Father Mathew   You heard the news?

Mark   I followed it.

Julie   He always follows the news.

Father Mathew   Really? What kind of news?

Julie   *Pointing to her t-shirt and that of Mark* Difficult to catch news.
Father Mathew   Of the bats?

Mark   Yes, bats you're killing Mathew for your old tower; your cheap tourist attraction.

Father Mathew   Easy Mark. The tower is not mine and the it is definitely not a cheap tourist attraction. As for the bats, we didn't kill any.

Julie   But they are suffering.

Father Mathew   Suffering?

Julie   All of them.

Father Mathew   What about our suffering? The suffering you see right here?

Mark   But you' re not chased or banished.

Father Mathew   We are in misery because of these new regulations and their fanatic followers.

Julie   I think he means you darling.

Father Mathew   It's easy to sell every environmentally attractive idea to civil servants sitting behind their discs.

Julie   Yes, he has been doing a lot of selling last year, aren't you Mark?

Father Mathew   To draw the most absurd protective policy and issue the most unrealistic laws.

38

Mark   You are not aware, as everybody else, of what bats are really doing for you Mathew, for our civilization and our planet.

Father Mathew   Don't start talking big Mark. You've always been good at that; save the world!

Mark   If I'm thinking big, you're thinking eternal. That's even worse! And wasn't mother thinking big?

Julie   You promised not to quarrel, Mark.

Mark   You're right Julie.

Julie   I guess your brother is trying to save the people and you're trying to save the world from the people. Am I right father?

They both look at her for a second, agreeing in their own way.

Mark   The problem is that you never ask yourself what these lovely creatures are really doing for us?

Father Mathew   You mean to us. Why don't you look around?

Mark   What you see is nothing if you compare it to the service they provide.

Father Mathew   All this is nothing?

Mark You don't provide enough facilities.

Julie You're right darling, I haven't seen any.

Father Mathew What facilities?

Mark All kind of facilities. Bats are no less than cows or horses. You only provide facilities for cows and horses because you profit of them; drink their milk, eat their meat and ride on their backs.

Father Mathew We can't ride bats.

Mark But you profit from every one of them and you can learn from each one of them.

Father Mathew Yes, they taught me to pray harder!

Mark Humans are ungrateful by nature.

Father Mathew And you belong to a more grateful race!

Mark Every bat is eating half of its weight of insects by tomorrow morning, to save you the trouble.

Father Mathew I don't eat insects, and I didn't ask them to do that for me.

Mark They are doing that on your behalf.

Father Mathew My behalf?

Mark You've just admitted it. You don't eat insects. You know what does this mean?

Julie He doesn't know Mark. Shall I tell him?

Mark Tell him Julie.

Julie Yes, I always love to tell this bit. It's fifty kilogram of insects in one summer!

Mark Not even Tom is capable of carrying such a job!

Julie Tom? Can he do that? Eat insects?

Mark Not really, but he has his way of dealing with plants and animals.

Father Mathew Tom is most knowledgeable man. And don't forget that he learned a lot of mother, whom you left when she was dying.
Mark *Avoiding the subject* Who cleans your wood?

Father Mathew *Reluctantly* Nobody Mark.

Mark Wrong. Bats clean all your wood, floors and ceilings, for nothing.

Julie Yes, always for nothing father. Gives you less trouble, saves you time and money father.

Father Mathew   I see.

Julie   Mark.

Mark   What?

Julie   Mosquitoes.

Father Mathew   Mosquitoes?

Mark   I almost forgot the mosquitoes.

Father Mathew   We don't have mosquitoes here.

Mark   And why do you think you don't have mosquitoes?

Julie   I don't see a single one.

Father Mathew   We don't miss them.
Mark   Of course you don't miss them, but where are your mosquitoes? What happened to them?

Father Mathew   We didn't kill any in case you suspect us.

Mark   No you don't kill mosquitoes, for bats do that for you.

Julie   They catch them, day in day out, without complain.

Mark   What else haven't you got?

Father Mathew   Right now I've got more than I can think of Mark!

Julie   Think father, have you got flies? Spiders?

Father Mathew   What do you mean? We don't have flies or spiders.

Julie   May be bugs father? Do you have bugs? Have you seen any?

Mark   Have you seen any insect invasion on your holy premises?

Father Mathew   Not that I noticed Mark.

Mark   You know why?

Julie   I know why.

Mark   I know you know darling.

Father Mathew   No we don't have insects, and I know why!

Mark   All these employers are doing the dirty job, without having one day off.

Julie   Working night shifts so you enjoy the day.

Father Mathew   You're wrong, they don't leave us in peace.

Julie Phantom workers.

Mark   In fact everyone should invite bats to his home.

Father Mathew They don't need an invitation.

Mark   Can you imagine what's going to happen when you kill all of them?

Father Mathew   We didn't kill one single bat Mark.

Mark   You prevent them from going back home, to their breeding premises, up in the tower. Can you imagine this place and your tower with millions of woodworms, mosquitoes, spiders, flies, bugs and the rest of the biblical plagues? Who is going to eat all that?

Julie   You know darling, maybe God killed first all the bats, and left the rest to nature. Flies and mosquitoes and the rest just multiplied. Do you think that's what happened in the plague story in the Bible father?

Father Mathew   No, God didn't need to kill bats. And don't play the saviour Mark. We can hardly cope.

Mark   You are the one with the saviours' dress for two thousand years. And look around! What did your mission accomplish on this planet?

44

Poverty and wars! You came, you failed, your time is over.

Father Mathew   And you are just the one who happens to have the solution for saving the planet, by securing bats droppings and all their filth, on any head at any time? Bats are our nightmare.

Long pause.

Father Mathew   Why are you here Mark?

Mark   To celebrate of course.

Father Mathew   Celebrate what?
Mark   The opening of the tower for the public.

Father Mathew   It took us quite a while to seal it.

Mark   It took you years of poisoning I guess. May be since I left.

Father Mathew   We didn't use poison, and you know why? It doesn't work.

Julie   You're right father, poison doesn't work. They come back, even in greater numbers.

Pause.

Father Mathew   Nice to have you back Mark.

Mark   I'm not back, I'm on a mission. You deliberately disturbed and destroyed the lovely resting places of these harmless creatures, and we are making everybody aware of this fact.

Father Mathew   You might also consider the dignity of our churches.

Mark   We have to accommodate nature. We shouldn't force it to change otherwise it hits back. You should have left them in peace. Soldiers are no longer in this mediaeval tower, and the church is getting less worshippers every day, and still you want to drive away the only creatures who happen to live in these deserted places.

Julie   That's why we're protesting.

Mark shakes the roll in his hand.

Father Mathew   What's that?

Mark   Tomorrow, before your morning prayers, this will be hanging from the top of the tower, and you'll have fifty protestors joining your celebrations.

Julie   On motorbikes.

Father Mathew   Protestors?

Julie   On motorbikes.

46

Father Mathew   I can't believe this. Nobody informed us of such demonstration.

Julie   *Patting her belly* We are family protesters father, aren't we darling? One doesn't need police escort to announce a family visit.

Mark   Exactly.

Father Mathew   I still can't believe it.

Mark   You better add this to what you believe Mathew. After all you're used to adding something every now and then.

Father Mathew   You didn't change.

Mark   I left this privilege to you.

Father Mathew   Why do you always have to be so revolutionary?

Mark   Oh, the firstborn, bookish wise brother is questioning us again!

Father Mathew   What are you trying to prove? To whom? To him?

Mark   Oh for your God's sake let us not start this again.

Father Mathew   He left and you turned against the world. You left to find him but you didn't. You know why? He never wanted to do anything with us, unless it was for his own benefit.

Mark   Don't start over him again. I didn't have a father since...

Father Mathew   Since mother was unwell.

Mark   Don't bring mother now. She has always been unwell because of him. And you've always been using this argument to be the captain of the ship. You just name it, and everyone says Amen.

Julie   They still say it darling.

Father Mathew   You've never taken the time to think Mark. You're always trying to catch him. If he's not there, then you are trying to catch something else, bats, or anything that's difficult to catch. You go after an ideal to convince yourself that you're on a mission!

Mark   At least I don't pretend it to be a holy mission like yours!

Julie   It's the journey not the destination. That's what you've said Mark, isn't it?

Father Mathew   It's both Julie.

Mark   May be because the journey was all I was left with. You were managing everything and everyone. Mother, the woodland, the house, the church, the tower, the yew, even the graveyard!

Father Mathew   I was forced to take care of everything after that he was gone with most of the assets. But the house is still up there.

Mark   It's your home.

Father Mathew   It's ours Mark. At least we are allowed to use it. It's still empty.

Julie   We did pass it, lovely lonely house.

She shifts feeling uncomfortable.

Father Mathew   *Notices, to Julie*   I think you should rest.

Julie   I think so too.

Mark   We're under your roof, sorry *Looks up, some droppings fall on his forehead, he wipes it with his hand* His roof!

Father Mathew   Would you like to use the house? I have the keys in here.

Mark   I don't think it is a good idea.

Father Mathew   I understand. You better take her to the meditation room. It's the only place I have here.

Julie Do we have to do that, meditate? You didn't say anything about meditating Mark?

Mark You love to watch nature Julie, that's meditating.

Father Mathew That's exactly what mother used to say.

Mark I'll bring the luggage.

Julie We don't need any tent in there?

Father Mathew You might need one. We've some meditating bunch up there.

Julie Meditating in a tent in the meditating room with some meditating bato. It should be very inspiring father!

Mark goes out left, Father Mathew goes out right to a side room, Julie walks outside, sees Tom reading in his book and seems busy with a basket in his hand, picking up things from the tree, putting them in the basket and to his mouth. He leaves it to go inside the tower with few working tools, she sits, looks at what in the basket, picks up something looks at it, smell it, puts it back, opens the book and starts reading and turning the pages, looks at the tree and the tower, reading, interested. In the meantime Mark has moved the luggage from the motorbike to the church. Tom comes back, looks alarmed, snatches the book and the basket from Julie.

Julie   Don't be angry Tom, I just wanted to see the tree. It's very beautiful but very old. How old is it?

Tom   Nobody knows, she thought it might be two thousand years.

Julie   Who is she?

Tom   The mistress.

Julie   You mean Dara, Mark's mother? Was she the mistress of the dead tree?

Tom   She's not dead.

Julie   Your mistress?

Tom   *Pause* The tree.

Julie   What else did Dara say?

Tom   The yew was their sacred book.

Julie   Whose sacred book?

Tom   The people who lived around here.

Julie   I see only a graveyard.

Tom   They lived, prayed and danced around the tree.

Julie   Is it sacred?

Tom   Yes, for everything went in cycles.

Julie   No wonder if they keep going in circles around the tree, everything goes in circles.

Tom   In cycles. The moon, the sun, winter and summer, but the tree stayed the same, never changed, and always with fruits and flowers.

Julie   Was it Dara's first church?

Tom   And last.

Julie   Didn't she go to this church?

Tom   She did, but she preferred big ones; woods, hills and fields.

Julie   It sounds like the Garden of Eden Tom.

Tom   And stayed with fruit and flowers.

Julie   Garden of Eden?

Tom   I haven't seen it.

Julie   I haven't seen it either but they say it's a place with fruits and flowers. What fruit does the tree have? It must be apples, the forbidden fruit.

Tom   No apples, but forbidden.

52

Julie You're not God to forbid it Tom.

Tom I don't forbid anything.

Julie And did Dara think it stands in the centre of the garden?
Tom For her the yew was the centre of the earth. Centre of all life.

Julie How do you know all that?

Tom She told me what others thought her.

Julie What was it you were arranging?

Tom I'm doing my job my lady. The tree is full of many things I have to take care of. Have you ever seen a yew before?

Julie I don't know, I'm not sure, I'm a city girl Tom, but it is fascinating. It was Mark who encouraged me to love nature.

Tom I think you loved nature before that.

Julie It might be true, but he taught me to see the meaning of it.

Tom We can only live according to its rules, and if we can't understand the rules, we should be happy to be able to live in its shadow.

Julie   Do you understand the rules Tom or live in the shadow?

Mark   Julie, you better come inside. We have to get up early.

Julie   Would you tell me more about Dara and the yew tomorrow Tom?

Tom does not hear, realising that, keeps looking at the tower and the tree, leaves with a curious look at Tom.

Act Two
The Following Day
Ash Wednesday

Scene One
Early Afternoon

Julie comes in looking at the tree, sits first on one bench, moves to the tree, she stretches herself on her back on the dead trunk, eyes closed, relaxing, patting her belly.

Boyd comes in.

Julie   It's quiet now Tom. Happy all visitors are gone?

Pause
Boyd sits on one of the benches.

You know Tom, it's better than the meditating room.

Boyd   It is a nice place to relax.

She opens her eyes without moving

Julie   Relax in a beautiful yew!

Boyd   But it's old and almost dead.

She sits

Julie   Old trees are beautiful.

Boyd Sometimes.

Julie Are you going up? It's almost closing time.

Boyd I'd like to take some photos before it is too late.

Julie Too late for what?

Boyd Oh, things can change, you know.

Julie I have a feeling nothing ever changes here.

Boyd More the reason to think of something new.

Julie I couldn't join them.

She pats her belly.

Boyd You came with friends?

Julie Yes. Fifty.

Boyd Fifty? For the tower?

Julie No, for the bats.

Boyd I understand they are all gone.

Julie And we want them back.

Boyd Back where?

Julie   Home.

Boyd   They're better off in the woods.

Julie   Do you see any woods left? They cleared the lot of it.

Boyd   That bunch of old trees was no woodland.

Julie   What would you call thirty acres of trees?

Boyd   How do you know there was woodland up there?

Julie   How do you know it was no woodland up there?

Boyd   Oh, it's a long story.

Julie   And a sad one.

Boyd   Tell me about your friends.

Julie   They're protestors.

Boyd   Were they all up there?

Julie   Most of them are gone now. They are in fact Mark's friends, the younger brother of the priest.
Boyd   I know he is the younger brother of Mathew. I am his father.

Julie The priest?

Boyd Mark, I mean both.

Julie I'm his wife, Mark's wife.

Boyd I didn't know he's married.

Julie And you're not dead.

Boyd Did he say that?

Julie No. He believes you've just disappeared somewhere in the cleared woodland.

Boyd I was away on business.

Julie Mark never liked to talk about this clearing business.

Boyd Dara, his mother died few years ago.

Julie Mark told me, was that before or after the clearing?

Boyd *Hesitant* I can't remember. We used to live at the end of the road.

Julie Mark didn't want to spend the night up there.
Boyd So many memories.

Pause

Tell me about the bats.

Julie Mark is protesting for what's going on.

Boyd And what's going on?

Julie You see, the ones that survived the attack on their nests up there, are now forced to take refuge in the this tree. They face settling problems.

Boyd Do they?

Julie Nothing wrong with the tree as a new home, but they were driven away from their original one. Would you like to be driven away from your home?

Boyd I prefer voluntarily departure.

She goes around the tree.

Julie Does the tree have a story?

Boyd Many.

Julie I love to listen to stories.

Boyd Why?

Julie So I can tell them to others.

Boyd I'm afraid the story of the tree has come to an end, and bats have to leave it very soon.

Julie You mean they have one-month notice?

Boyd Not even a week notice.

Julie O dear, I better tell Mark. He might protest for the tree as well.

She heads to the church when Father Mathew comes out.

Father Mathew How are you Julie? I hope you did sleep well.

Julie Who wouldn't in a meditation room, father!

Father Mathew Any inspiration?

Julie The tent prevented it.

Father Mathew Have you seen Mark?

Julie He's still up there. Poor Mark; he has to find the bats a new home.

Father Mathew seems not understanding what she means.
She goes inside.
Boyd comes from behind the yew

Boyd Good afternoon Mathew.

Father Mathew God Gracious!

Boyd It's only me, your father.

60

Father Mathew   I wasn't expecting to see you.

Boyd   It seems you've got a family reunion today.

Father Mathew   And you didn't want to miss it. What brings you now?

Boyd   It's a nice occasion for some photos of the tower and the tree up there.

Father Mathew   To what we owe the sudden interest?

Boyd   I've always been interested.

Father Mathew   Should I take that as a threat?

Boyd   I'm truly pleased the tower is open now.

Father Mathew   The tower has never been your subject of interest.

Boyd   You might be right. But the tree....

Father Mathew   What about it today?

Boyd   It stands in the way.

Father Mathew   You mean it stands in your way?

Boyd   It blocks the road to the developed area.

Father Mathew   Is this the name for mother's woodland?

Boyd   I thought we've put all that behind us.

Father Mathew   Fifteen years ago you destroyed the heath.

Boyd   It was wasteland that we use now for public facilities. The village needed modern impulse.

Father Mathew   Then you cleared the woodland to build your exclusive houses.

Boyd   It was no woodland Mathew

Father Mathew   It was for mother.

Boyd   We needed homes for the young generation.

Father Mathew   Greed homes. And now the tree. The yew is old.

Father Mathew   Exactly. It had its time. It's shapeless, dry and it has to give way to the road.

Father Mathew   Is this your argument?

Boyd   Look at it. The trunks are hollow and shed most depressing shadows. Not only that. It's blocking the entrance to the tower, the church and the graveyard.

Father Mathew   You want me to believe that you're suddenly concerned about the cultured, the believers and even the dead?

Boyd   We better settle this in a friendly way Mathew.

Father Mathew   It is her tree.

Boyd   Dara left me the land.

Father Mathew   To take care of.

Boyd   And I did.

Father Mathew   By clearing and selling.

Boyd   It's too late to talk about all that now.

Father Mathew   The yew is a landmark. It stood here before there was a village.

Boyd   People come to pray in a church now. They don't come to sit around the tree any more.

Father Mathew   People don't need to sit around a tree to prove its value.

Boyd   Are you telling me it has a religious value?

Father Mathew   Among other things. And yes, it had a religious value for mother.

Boyd   I'm sorry to say, your mother had no religion.

Father Mathew   You'll never understand. She loved and respected nature, and the tree was the centre.

Boyd   She was drown to it by some undefined power. She imagined herself a priestess of some kind, and treated the tree as a goddess.

Father Mathew   The land you took was her universe, and she had the deepest respect for the power that's hidden in it, and in the universe. You destroyed her world.

Boyd   She didn't believe in your Bible.
Father Mathew   Nature was her church and the universe was her bible. And in case you don't know, the Bible, my Bible, celebrates God's divine creation.

Boyd   And what was the tree? The altar?

Father Mathew   You shouldn't talk like that. Your sarcasm, narrow mindedness and belittling never stopped. It kept going on and on and on. It made her sick.

Pause.

Boyd   I tried to understand Mathew, but at the end...

Father Mathew You left.

Boyd Your mother left us first. Her whole life was her natural beliefs. What do you want me to do? In the beginning I thought it's only a strange hobby. But it turned out to be much more than that. She didn't care about you or Mark.

Father Mathew She simply embraced the natural world as manifestation of her deep devotion to God. She did what she thought is right for herself and for us. She was always around.

Boyd And you kept her company, watching whatever she was doing.
Father Mathew She didn't want you to leave and she was dying when Mark left. And now he is back.

Boyd Mark had that spirit to fight. That's why he left. Not to find me, but to fight me. He wanted to do what you and your mother couldn't do.

Father Mathew Was that the reason you left him to fight your ghost? Alone? Now he is fighting the battle of the bats up there!

Boyd Let us not discuss Mark now. I'll talk to him later. The tree is the problem.

Father Mathew The tree has always been your problem. You're jealous of it. You think it stole mother and now it stands literary in your way.

Boyd   You're still sensitive to anything related to Dara.

Father Mathew   Sensitive? The fact is that she embarrassed you. You were ashamed of how she dressed, how she used to wear her hair, what she was cooking, reading, thinking or writing. Ashamed of people coming for healing. You never accepted her.

Boyd   She was a complex mix of many tendencies and eccentrics. I have to admit, I've never been able to understand her.

Father Mathew   You know why? Because she was larger than life figure, and difficult to be put in a frame, and that was disturbing. You were not living close to God and you were not a problem, and she was living close to nature and she was a problem.

Boyd   Yes, for the one week she was fasting for Easter and the other week she was feasting for some natural phenomena! Celebrating New Year in October and setting bonfires in June.

Father Mathew   Good reasons for leaving a family.

Boyd   No. I guess she was standing too close to everybody and everything and that drove me away; making me not want to be close to anyone or any thing.

Father Mathew Not even your own sons?

Boyd I love you, both of you, but I admit I couldn't cope with her world.

Father Mathew But you are coping so good with her property that you sold, to build your own new world.

Boyd It was her leaving the land without any concrete use.

Father Mathew She was perfectly in harmony with the land. It was her property and nature was her means of understanding what lies beyond our senses.

Boyd It was emptiness, vagueness and lack of purpose that drove me mad.

Father Mathew Our life was full of beautiful things that you failed to see. Her purpose was to enjoy the day, the present, and yours was to accumulate and expand and live for tomorrow. For you, nature meant money.

Boyd Let us not talk about Dara now.

Father Mathew Let us not talk about Mark now, let us not talk about Dara now. Now means never.

Pause.

Boyd   Look Mathew, I know you need some branches of the tree for Palm Sunday. I can take care of that.

Father Mathew   We burn some branches after Palm Sunday, to use a year later on Ash Wednesday.

Boyd   Ash Wednesday.

Father Mathew   Today.
Boyd   Ash Wednesday, Holy Thursday, Good Friday, White Saturday. All these names. I guess it's a nice way of keeping people busy.

Father Mathew   Would it make any difference if I tell you they have spiritual meanings?

Boyd   No. You know why? Because deep down in your heart the ideas of your mother are profoundly rooted more than the beliefs of this church. The tree stands taller in your heart than any cross in the world.

Father Mathew   You're free to think what you want.

Boyd   In all honesty Mathew, what was behind this decision to become a priest? Was it shame?

Father Mathew   Shame?

Boyd   I think you were ashamed of sticking around this place, so you decided to worship inside. I guess it was your way of coping with reality. But still you had to be, like Dara, at the head of the worshipers!

Father Mathew   Was it also shame that drove you from home to manipulate the land?

Boyd   No. Anger drove me away. Anger is the motor behind achieving most difficult dreams.

Pause.

Let us not talk about all that today Mathew. You are celebrating your tower. I've just come to inform you that a decision is about to be taken to remove the tree. I would like to take few photos to document that the tree was blocking the path.

Father Mathew   We are good in that. Document, and try to remember after destruction. Relive the past!

Boyd   The past lives in documentaries, wouldn't you agree?

Father Mathew   The past lives in what is alive. The tree is alive.

Boyd   I'm going up to see Mark. I couldn't have planned it better.

Father Mathew   On top of a medieval tower, looking upon a thousand year old yew, after celebrating Ash Wednesday mass? No, you couldn't have planned it better!

Boyd   The past seems very much alive.

Father Mathew   Indeed. It's only you who thinks it is dead.

Act Two
Scene two
Same day
One Hour Later

Up stage centre forms the top of the tower while down stage left is the green around the yew.

Voices of children playing, they come playing around hide and seek with some vague ash cross on their foreheads. They go back in and behind the church.
Kevin enters, looks around and seeing nobody he disappears in the grove, comes back with the old book, goes around the tree where nobody can see him, sits on a bench and begins to read.

On top of the tower.
Mark comes in, starts taking off his demonstration banner that hands outside the tower. Couple of his friends are helping him. They head downstairs.
Sound of motorbikes leaving.
Martin comes in.

Martin   Can I help?

Mark   Did Mathew ask you to come up here?

Handing him some banners and other items to put in a plastic bag.

Martin   No. I saw the motorbikes leaving. It was exciting all these people up here, and the motorbikes down there.

Short pause.

You like bats.

Mark Not really.

Martin Why are you doing it?

Mark It's a matter of principle. Either you respect nature or you hate yourself.

Martin You demonstrate for other things?

Mark I demonstrate for life, and they are not things.

Martin I'm sorry.

Mark Can you take these down?

Martin Sure.

He lingers.

Mark You don't have to take me down.

Martin Are you leaving today?

Mark Yes, why?

Martin I was thinking you might tell me more about other thin .. sorry, life…living.. you know, what you do.

Mark I'm afraid we'll be leaving after dinner.

Martin Are you planning to come back?

Mark I don't think so. I might, in few years time.

Martin goes down.
In the meantime, near the yew, Julie comes quietly, making sure nobody is seeing her, sneaks into the groves of the tree, sits, sleeps on one of the long arms of the tree, gets up, goes inside, comes back with a book. May comes in, goes to Julie, sits and looking closely at the book in Julie's hands.

May Did he give it to you?

Julie No, I couldn't resist going in there.

May We're not allowed to sneak in there.

Julie It's a tree not a home.

May It is for Tom.

Julie Can we really believe all what's written in it?

May It's Tom's world, he believes it.

Julie No, it is our world, a world that it's all gone but still in front of our eyes.

May What do you mean? Did he write all that?

Julie Tom? No, it's Dara.

May Who is Dara?

Near the yew, Tom comes in from the church with the children, and start taking down all festivities and balloons. The children have some vague grey sign of a cross on their foreheads.
Tom sees May and Julie reading in his books. He goes to them, setting, chatting and picking up one of the books explaining. Kevin comes in. Tom gives him few papers to read.

In the meantime on top of the tower Boyd reaches the top of the tower, stops watching Mark for a moment and catching his breath. Mark still busy with his work

Mark The party is over.

Boyd I didn't come to demonstrate.

Mark You're right. Land developers are usually interested in something more attractive than bats.

Boyd How are you Mark?

Mark I'm afraid I'll have to disappoint you. Still no time for arguing if that's what you were hoping for.
Boyd We never had time to talk things over.

Pause.
Mark goes on collecting his demonstrating material and Boyd leans on the wall looking over the tree and the church.

It's nice to see you Mark.

Mark I hope you don't expect to hear the same.

Boyd You have a lovely wife.

Mark I saw you talking to her.

Boyd It's an interesting place to talk. May be it's time to turn a new page.

Mark Turning pages is a very heavy task you know? Besides I'm sure we're here for very different reasons. What brings you here today?

Around the tree.
Julie, Tom, Kevin and May sit around the tree, while children are busy collecting items, laughing, playing, bringing things inside the church, pricking balloons now and then.

Tom You should promise not to go inside again.

Julie I'm sorry Tom, I wanted to read about the tree before we leave.

Kevin And I have a question.

Tom It's hopeless to keep them safe.

He goes to the tree, comes back with couple of books. The three look puzzled.

Julie How many do you have in there Tom?

Kevin A whole library!

May And you wanted to read his bible!

Kevin Why did people come to the tree Tom?

Tom Long, long ago it was the only evergreen tree in whole of England. And it was a symbol of reincarnation.

May Reincarnation?

Julie He means the dead becomes alive again, isn't it Tom?

Tom Everything becomes alive again, and now we say resurrection.

Kevin Like Jesus.

May I know what is resurrection Kevin, but why?

Tom You see, the branches grow down into the ground to form new stems, then rise up round the old one, separate but linked together, you see, you can't distinguish which is the old and which is the new.

Julie It gives birth to a new baby tree? Can you distinguish them Tom?

Tom Yes.

Kevin   You didn't say why the people used to come here.

Tom   To celebrate the New Year. The thirty first of October was the beginning of the year, called Samhain, when the harvest ends, and the dark half of the year begins.

Julie   It's Halloween we celebrate on the thirty first of October.

Tom   That's what it's called now. Feast of all saints.

May   But why come to the tree?

Tom   I'll explain it to you. Read, read.

May   You said you will explain Tom?

Tom   Yes, read, read!

Kevin   "The tree is thriving with life, and keeps renewing itself." You've just said that Tom.

Tom   Read, read!

Julie   "It is associated with immortality, regeneration, rebirth and access to the otherworld and our ancestors."

Pause.

I don't like this "otherworld and ancestors" part of it Tom.

She looks a bit troubled, she closes the book but Tom hastens to open it again for her and signs her to read.

"It can live as much as four thousand year." Who would believe this Tom!

Tom   Go on Kevin, read.

Kevin   "It is a slow-growing tree, that is why it has a tight-grained wood, used in the past for spears, small hunting bows and longbows used in the Middle Ages".

Julie   The middle ages? I wish I've lived in the middle ages.

Pause.
Did she write all of this?

Tom   Yes. She was always around and there in the woods, listening, noting, reading and writing.

May   *Looking closely at one of the books* Look at these border paintings. They look pagan. Was she pagan?

Tom   What do you mean pagan? Of course not!

Kevin   They are Celtic.

May   Was she Celtic?

Julie   They are Anglo-Saxon.

Kevin   Then she was Anglo Saxon.

Julie   Kevin, Dara died few years ago.

Kevin   You're right, not Anglo Saxon.

Julie   But the paintings are Anglo Saxon.

Kevin   How do you know?

Julie   I had some art history courses couple of years ago.

Tom   They are Roman.

Kevin   You don't want to say she was Roman?

Julie   I think they are a mix of all that. You know why? It is full of fish symbols, snakes, knots, and metric lines.

May   Shall we read what's written here?

Tom   You read, I'll do couple of things in there.

Tom goes to the church.
The four of them sit, each a book in hand, relaxed, with voices of children in the background.
Julie goes in the tree, comes back with another book and a small basket, starts eating some red fruits from the basket,

puts the basket back in the tree, and sits reading in the book

On top of the tower.

Boyd Let's not talk about the reason of my visit.

Mark End conversation.

Boyd We can talk about your wife, Julie, and the twins she expects.

Mark A bit odd to develop sudden interest after so many years. Don't you think so?

Pause.
Boyd It was a successful protest. Your protesters did their best. I mean talking with visitors and worshippers.

Mark It wouldn't protect bats from the barbaric actions of Mathew.

Boyd I'm not sure if Mathew's actions are barbaric, but what you're doing is certainly noble. Securing a home for bats.

Mark Noble? Have you seen the church benches?

Boyd No I haven't. Should I?

Mark I wonder if see them you would still call my action noble. But I forgot, you're not religious, so you might consider it after all noble, just to tease God.

Pause.
Fishing packing demonstration articles, looking him strait in the eye

What was it that brought you here?

Boyd   Some unfinished business.

Mark   I should have known. It has always been unfinished business that brought you back. Your last unfinished business visit did finish mother.

Boyd   Let's not talk about the past.

Mark   Considering we don't have a shared present, and I detest a shared future, we are only left with the past.

Pause.

Money was behind your first unfinished business, to destroy the heath, then came the second, the woodland.

Boyd   It was no woodland. I know you were young when I left, but I had my reasons.

Mark   Your reasons, always you. Have you ever thought of my reasons? Why did I leave?

Boyd It was too much of a burden, sick mother worshipping around a tree, and a brother who suddenly discovers that he wants to be a priest. It was the shame and unease I believe that drove you away.

Mark You're right, it was shame, but not of mother or Mathew. I was ashamed of you. You were the reason I left. I hated you for leaving us, but I hated you more for your hunger for money. I hated the smell of money in my hand since. Every time I touch money was like shaking hand with you. I became ashamed of every penny I earn. The smell of you, the smell of money is always in my head. You left with our money and by doing so you poisoned every penny in the world that I could be earning. I had to live of nature not of money! And you think that we can turn a new page on top of this tower?

Boyd Mathew is right. I was the reason you went away.

Mark I went away not after you, but to be away from you.

Boyd Did your mother know?

Mark Is it relevant now? The answer is no. She died thinking I went on a crusade to bring you home. Would that ease your conscious?

Boyd Look Mark, I didn't plan to meet you, I didn't know you are here. I just wanted to take some photos of the tower and the yew.

Mark Why now?

Boyd *Looking down from the tower, thinking* Julie might tell you.

Mark Tell me what? Does she know something that I don't know?

Boyd No, I mean, yes, she wanted to talk to you.

Mark She can't come up here. What did you say to her?

Boyd I was just chatting with her about the tree and how it grew.

Mark And?

Boyd It blocks the entrance.

Mark In case you didn't notice, the tree has been blocking the entrance before I was born. It didn't grow one centimetre last twenty years. Ask Tom.

Boyd Oh, it looks as if it grew in thickness.

Mark It's just a reaction humans usually get when they start developing a sense of aggressiveness towards nature.

Boyd   I never realised that with such difficulty one can pass the entrance without getting scratched.

Mark   Right. Passing the entrance for years was not enough to notice.

Boyd   Yews might not grow fast but their dead and hollow trunks manage to block entrances of churches and towers.

Mark   *Looking over the yew* So that's what you think the yew is?

Boyd   I'm afraid so. A dead, ugly, hollow trunk.

Mark   And that's why you wanted very much to climb up the tower to take photos of this dead, ugly, hollow trunk?

Boyd   Before it is too late, it might fall or disappear.

Mark   Disappear? Like you did?

Boyd   But I'm back.

Mark   That's what a yew exactly does. It comes back. It grows again after being seemingly dead for years. You share some similarity!

Boyd   I didn't realise that.

Mark   The tree is a perfect ancient living yew. What's your problem?

Boyd   The graveyard deserves a cheerful sight.

Mark   And who is depressed here, the living or the dead?

Boyd   Nobody is depressed.
Mark   Good to know that.

Boyd   We've never managed to have a decent conversation.

Mark   Maybe because you never manage to tell the truth.

Boyd   The truth is that I'll be removing the yew.

Mark   Is that the truth or half-truth?

Boyd   It stands in the way of widening the main road to the town. The tower needs bigger entrance as well.

Mark   And of course the decision didn't take in consideration that it was more than a tree for mother. And it stands in the centre of what was our playground.

Boyd   She left you playing around the dead.

Mark   Believe me, the dead are everywhere.

Boyd   Memories shouldn't stand in the way of development. I try to bring more life to this village.

Mark   What about the evicted bats from the tower that settled in it?
Boyd   They will find another tree.

Mark   Thanks to you there isn't a single one left around here. Something has to be done.

Boyd   You can't do a thing Mark.

Mark   Mother used to say nature has its say and has its way, and according to Mathew, God does miracles.

Boyd   I doubt it, since I didn't share your mother's beliefs and the tree has got such a non-Christian history!

Around the tree.

Julie   May, Kevin, you should hear this   *Reading* "It helps healing, protects against evil."

May   I don't understand, how can this tree *do* anything!

Kevin   Spooky.

Tom goes in the tree and brings a bundle of cloth and opens it, and gives some papers to May to read.

May "The wood is easy to carve and has a golden orange red core. It was used in the past for making spoons, bowls and the lute. And it was used to make sacred articles." What's sacred articles?
Tom starts putting some items as spoons and wooden plates and small jar and cups, and they all sit on the ground around the tree to marvel at the way they are carved.
Tom starts with clipping the tree.

Tom I have to finish what I started yesterday. It doesn't look good. But you go ahead. I am listening.

Julie Listening?

Tom I am listening to Dara. She read it hundreds of times.

Julie *Reading and her voice overlaps and becomes Dara's voice.* "It helps us overcome our fear of death and it brings us peace in our lives. Death marks the ending of something, but it is a new beginning as well. Sometimes things need to die before the new can begin. To understand rebirth we need to see beyond our limitations."
What a philosophical nonsense! But it is a very beautiful nonsense.

She stretches in calmness on the dead trunk of the tree.

It might not be all nonsense!

On top of the tower.

Mathew Enters, catching his breath.

Mark Hail to the hero!

Father Mathew Tom is the hero. He worked for months up here.

Mark Your name will be written in the eternal records of this old tower. Mathew, son of Dara, priestess of the yew, and Boyd the pride of the cleared woodland, symbol of the developed world, and last but not least the one who managed to rid the world of the yew, Mathew did manage, after three hundred years, to reopen the medieval tower for the public, after launching a fierce battle on the bats, and defeating all the enemies that occupied the decayed walls for so long.

Father Mathew *Laughing* And the council did agree the sealing without harming the bats.

Mark You mean you've been merciful enough to make them homeless? Exile them?

Father Mathew We still have them in the church.

Mark Even worse! Most unethical! To get the support of the council to clear the tower for tourists, but not the church for worshippers! Has your God lost his support among council members?

88

Father Mathew   We have to finance sealing the church by means of the tower, if we get enough visitors.

Boyd   That's a start.

Mark   And the yew?

Father Mathew   I disagree with this wild plan of cutting it.

Mark   And I can't believe the reason is widening the entrance.

Father Mathew   What do you mean?

Boyd   *To Mark*   You're always ...

Mark   Why don't you tell us the real reason?

Father Mathew   He said he wants to develop the area around the tower and the graveyard. Isn't that true?

Boyd   It is true.

Mark   But not the whole truth, am I right?

Boyd   Ok. The yew will be used in experimental treatment for cancer.

Mark   Aha, here comes part of the truth. This yew forms only a tiny part of an experiment on one single patient.

Boyd Correct. One single patient.

Mark And you would still have to find another five or six yews as old as this one, to provide you with the needed stuff for this experiment on one single patient?

Boyd Yes, for one single patient who is badly in need of it. Believe me every patient is in great need of it.

Father Mathew You want to cut the yew for research?

Boyd I need. I mean they need a great deal of old yews.

Mathew Who are they?

Boyd The doctors, the researchers.

Father Mathew Did you know about this?

Mark That's why they're cutting every old yew they come across.

Father Mathew Is this your new business?

Boyd It's not a business. It is supporting a research. I have a very personal reason to ...

Mark What personal reason? You mean money reason. You don't have to possess a great deal of intelligence to figure out that it wouldn't take us long to find ourselves living in a world cleared of all yews.

Boyd A completely new park of yews is planned. I take one and get you a whole park! I only wish I did that few years ago!

Mathew What difference would that have made?

Boyd It would, it might have saved...

Mark The one single patient of yours? What a noble act! It takes a century to grow a yew as thick as your fist.

Boyd First the bats and now the yews. What's your next battle Mark? Your revolution wouldn't reshape the past.

Mark You're right. But it might reshape the future and save the bats, the tree, my world and the world I want for my children.

Boyd What about the patients and their sufferings? A world without progress is not worth living. And who knows maybe in ten or hundred years we come to discover that bats have medical values, so that we'll go hunting bats instead of hating them.

Father Mathew A world where nature has no maker is without a purpose. It's a world that fails to understand the value of the human nature. So long as the likes of both of you reject the real purpose of mankind, we'll always have the two extremes; the giants like you, who regard themselves a super power, selfish, hunting for money, while you idealises the created material world. Both of you refuse to see beyond. It's neither money nor material that counts.

Boyd We are not in the church Mathew, keep your sermons to those who believe in it. Both of you are defending a world that is far too idealistic, gone, has never been so beautiful as you imagine it to be. The eternal coming kingdom of God, and the beautiful golden old days. Eden is not to be lived on this earth, but not in the world to come either. It's all imagination. Bad dreams. Get real.

Mark These bats had to find alternative places other than the tower. And you cleared the neighbouring woodland and want to cut the only tree left. Where would they go?

Boyd We can't continue living in the jungle era Mark.

Mark Don't you understand? They are now sleeping in the groves of the yew you want to destroy.

Boyd The order is about to be given.

Mark   And I'm not leaving the yew. What do you intend to do Mathew?

Father Mathew   What do you expect me to do? I can only pray!

Tom is still busy clipping the yew and the children are heard in the background playing, Kevin and May are sitting near the tree, with books in hand.

May   *Reading and her voice overlaps and becomes Dara's voice* "Mourners used to carry branches of yew which are thrown in the grave under the body or on top of the coffin."
You think that's why they throw flowers on coffins now? They can't find yews!

Julie   *Reading* "Now thousands of years later, it is providing a possibility for saving cancer patients."
You hear that? It kills and cures. It sounds very godly!

Kevin   *Reading* "And the arrows were tipped with poison taken from the yew."

Tom   The entire tree is poisonous; wood, needles and seed. Even the dust produced from sanding wood is poisonous. People have to take care working with yews.

Julie shifts, cleans her hands in her clothes, looks at her hands.

Kevin   How come you're not dead Tom? You're always busy with cutting and cleaning.

Tom   You can eat the he red fleshy part of the fruit, and birds eat them. They get rid of the hard seeds in their droppings.

Kevin   So that's what you are eating the whole time.

May   Listen to this   *Reading, in the meantime Julie behind her has risen, feeling bad almost fainting* "Children should never chew the seeds of the green shoots, because poison is quickly absorbed and causes vomiting and painful diarrhoea and collapse. The first hour after eating the fruits is very crucial".

Julie its on the ground, lies, in pain, begins to vomit.
Tom hurries to the bell.

Kevin   How much did you eat Julie?

Julie   *Fainting*   I can't remember.

Kevin   *Picks up the book again* "The lethal dose for an adult is estimated to be fifty grams of the leaves, but as few as four of the seeds may prove fatal for a child."

Julie   Oh, my babies! *Faints*

94

Tom rings the bell, loud, they put hands on their ears and shout to each other Children come to see what's going on. Black out.

On top of the tower.

Father Mathew I told him, it's only for Sundays.

Mark It must be Sunday down there.

Boyd Tom is old.

Father Mathew Tom is quite alert.

The three of them look from the tower

Mark It's Julie, something is wrong.

Darkness, bell goes on ringing

Act Two
Scene Three
Five Days Later

Julie, Mark, Boyd sit in the church with the children and other people with their backs to audience, a small coffin in front of the altar, a child carriage beside Julie. Tom is busy digging a grave in the far left. Father Mathew is busy with the funeral rituals, we hear only the children whispering, wearing their Chinese hats. Candles.

May   Did you notice?

Matt   What?

May   Not one drop on the baby coffin!

Kevin   And not on any of the people.

Martin   How do you know?

Elizabeth   Nobody's shaking his head.

Martin   Why is that?

Kevin   Bats are mourning.

May   You sound like Tom!

Annemarie   You think they know?

Martin   They hear what's going on.

Matt What do you think of the ash?

May What about it?

Matt You think father Mathew put it on the baby?

May I don't know.

Matt I think he did.

Joe But it's only a baby.

Annemarie And I think he didn't repent.

Joe Why?

Annemarie He can't talk.

Elizabeth You think this happened because she was a city girl?

Kevin I don't think so.

Elizabeth I'm a city girl.
Matt No you're not. You don't live in the city.

Elizabeth It sounds nice.

Martin City girls are ignorant. They eat wrong stuff.

May You didn't know either!

Martin But we didn't eat it.

Martin Mark should have never brought her here.

Joe He wanted to have a party up the tower with all his motorbikes.

Annemarie I like her.

Joe I like her baby.

Kevin We all do, she was talking to Tom, and nobody noticed…

May I hate the old man. It's all his fault.

Matt It's not his fault.

Elizabeth He wanted to cut the tree and sell it in pieces.

Joe To sick people.

Annemarie To kill them all? Is he mad?

Martin Only crazy.

Kevin We should keep an eye on Tom.

Annemarie Why?

Kevin   I want to know how is he going to detect the bats in the church.

Elizabeth   He keeps his headphones on.

Kevin   He said horses are the most sensitive animals to this poison. They can die in minutes if they eat young shoots.

May   Would you stop it Kevin?

Joe   I have never seen a dead horse.

Kevin gets a paper of his pocket.

Kevin   He said one gram of leaves….

May   Shut up Kevin.

Joe   How many did she eat?

Elizabeth   Enough to kill one baby.

Kevin   Pigs also…

May   Why are you so much into this fruit Kevin? You give me the creeps.

Kevin   They are facts and we better know them.

May   I don't care about all this, I'll leave after school.

Elizabeth   To be a city girl?

May starts hitting her with her hat.

Act Two
Scene Four
Palm Sunday
Thirty-Six Days Later
Afternoon

Children are coming from church. There are Palm Sunday decorations made of yew branches in their hands, around their heads and on the door of the church as a cross. They start grabbing yew leaves and branches and pile them up in the area between the yew and the tower, preparing for a fire. They are in the background the whole of the scene playing. Mathew comes with couple of small branches in hand. Mark comes from the tower.

Mark Where is Julie?

Father Mathew You know Mark. She is visiting Ashley.

Mark Would she ever be able to leave?

Father Mathew It's only one month, give her a bit more time.

Pause.

He didn't show up since…

Mark Did you really expect him to do that?

Father Mathew I don't know, but what happened was not his fault, nobody's fault.

101

Mark   And what do you think is going to happen now?

Father Mathew   He might come on Easter, next week.

Mark   Claiming the last piece of land and cutting the tree?

Father Mathew   We can't do anything about it. You might not be around any way.

Mark   I am ready to leave, but Jolie...

Father Mathew I have to admit I got used to the three of you.

Mark   Julie has to go to work in few weeks time, and my unpaid leave ends next month. We have nothing to do here.

Father Mathew   Julie has been quite busy with herbs and plants in Tom's plot.

Mark   It's a nice hobby. Not making a living.

Father Mathew   I know. But it's a positive way of mourning. We thank God she is fine and April is a great child.

Boyd enters

Mark   Speaking of the devil.

Father Mathew   Easy Mark.

Boyd   I thought I might find you here.

Father Mathew   We've just finished mass.

Boyd   Where is Julie?

Mark   What do you want her for?

Father Mathew   She is back in a moment.

Boyd places a file on a bench and starts looking at some papers.

Mark   You could have posted it. It would have saved you the trouble.

Boyd   I'm afraid I needed to bring it myself Mark.

Mark   And you need us all as witness.

Julie comes pushing the baby carriage. Wearing hair scarves on her loos hair, long dress, with shawl around her bare arms. Clearly her appearance is different than the city girl on the motorbike behind Mark. For a moment she walks with her back to them.
Boyd looks, taken back and whispers
Boyd   Dara!

Mathew and Mark look at each other.
Julie turns, stops for a moment and goes towards them.

Boyd How are you Julie?

Julie I'm fine, thank you.

Boyd And how is April?

Julie Sleeping.

Boyd You look like ...you look quite well.

Mark Yes, she looks lovely.

Julie *Touching her dress and shawl* I found these in the attic.

Boyd The attic. I understand you're staying in the house now. And you like taking care of Tom's plot?

Julie Who told you that?

Boyd Tom of course. Where is he by the way? He said he would be here.

Father Mathew What does Tom has to do with it?

Julie With what?

Mark This is ridiculous!

Julie Don't start Mark.

Tom comes from behind the tower, places more branches near the children.

Here he is!

Boyd   How are you Tom?

Tom still wearing headphones, nods.

Tom   Back again?

Boyd   You can't get rid of me so quickly Tom. Not yet! You should hear what I am about to say. Julie would you please sit down?

She sits, Tom sits beside her.

Father Mathew   May be you can explain what's going on?

Boyd a bit embarrassed

Mark   It's the usual unfinished business. We all know about the land and the yew, is there anything else?

Boyd   You're right Mark, it is about the land and the yew. Julie, may I hand you the legal documents of your property. You are the new owner of the land over there, the house, and the land around the yew.

Tom   And the yew?

Boyd And the yew of course Tom.

They all look at each other.
Tom can't help a big smile

It is simple. Julie owns this land and she is free to decide what to do with it.

Julie But why?

Boyd I think you know why Julie. You love it here and for more than one reason. I'm sure you, and Mark, would be able to do something with these ten acres. After all, there was this plan for a yew park or may be a natural herbal centre.

Mark This is what you want her to do for you?

Father Mathew It's what Julie would like to do Mark.

Tom Right.

Mark What is right now Tom?

Tom Your father. For a change!
Julie But I can't accept it.

Boyd Why?

Julie You should give it to Mathew and Mark.

Father Mathew In fact I see the logic behind this Julie.

Mark Why you always see what others don't see!

Father Mathew If we get it, we would reject it. It's far too painful to regard a gift now!

Mark I don't want anything from him.

Father Mathew That's exactly what I mean.

Boyd That settles it then.

Julie What about the experiment you needed the tree for?

Boyd It was too late to begin with, but I'm sure they will be saving other patients in the future.

Silence

I think I should be going now.
He hands Julie the papers

Julie When would you be coming back?

Boyd I don't know Julie, I'm not sure if I will be able to do that in the near future.

Julie I hope you do.

Boyd You take care of April. Goodbye Mathew. Mark, take care.

Boyd leaves

Mark Can anyone tell me what's going on?

Father Mathew Quite unexpected.

Mark What are you going to do Julie?

Julie I'm going back to the plot, I need to write few things down.

Mark I mean what are you going to do with all that?

Julie We are already doing Mark!

Julie turns, comes back

Julie Father Mathew, would it be possible to baptise April here?

Mark Here?
Father Mathew I have to think about it Julie.

Julie leaves

Tom Right.

Mark She doesn't seem surprised. You think she knew something?

Tom   She knew something, but not what your father have just said.

Mark   What?

Tom   You better ask her.

Father Mathew   *To Mark* I have a feeling he is not telling the whole truth again.

Mark   He's always hiding something. *To Tom* Shall I give you a hand sealing the church Tom?

Tom looks suspiciously.

Mark   You gave Julie the books and she wants to publish them, don't you trust me?

Tom smiles in yes and no way
Mathew and Mark leave.
Julie and May comes in.

May   And April kept quiet during mass.
Julie   She falls asleep on the sound of singing in there.

May   Are you leaving after Easter?

Julie   I don't think so. We have to see for planting the park. We might call it Dara's Park.

May   I would like to help you.

Julie I thought you are going away.

May I changed my mind, I'm going to the local academy.

Julie That would be great May.

May Shall I take April for a short walk?

Julie You do that.

May pushes the carriage around the tree and the tower.

Tom *To Julie* You don't have to go to this class Julie.

Julie I think I have Tom. Sign language is not difficult, and it would be easier for both of us!

Tom And the trees?

Julie Next week Tom. They are only two feet high! You choose the best for Ashley up there.

Tom Don't you worry, we put it right beside him. He's not alone.

Julie No one is really alone Tom. I have a feeling that Boyd wouldn't come back, but I don't know why. Was it his guilty feelings that made him do that?

Tom No, he really wanted you to have the land.

She gives him a hand with what he is doing. Martin comes in. Martin comes in and starts helping them. Mark comes with his motorbike

Martin   I heard you might be staying a bit longer.

Mark   And I you have more than one question.

Martin   Yes.

Mark   Good, you'll get the answer while helping me.

In the meantime, the rest of the children are gone behind the tower and the church.
Mark   Who would have thought?

Father Mathew   You said nature has its say and has its way.

Mark   Mother used to say that. But was it really nature?

Father Mathew   I'm no sure.

Mark   Do you think we can really start a real natural centre for a living?

Father Mathew   I think you know it is what both of you wanted last few years. And if you love doing it, you succeed in it.

Mark   I think Julie is ahead of me grasping the situation.

Father Mathew   She is not ahead or behind, she only takes things as they happen.

Mark leaves. Mathew goes to children

Father Mathew   Oh children, we don't need all that.

Branches are burning.
Father Mathew and children stand, back to audience, watching.
Julie is reading. Tom disappears in the tree, comes back puts the other three books beside Julie
Kevin comes, picks a book. Both Julie and Kevin start talking to each other, and look through the books, exchanging papers.
Julie picks another book.
Sound of burning branches mixes with the sound of Dara's voice.

"It assists us to heal the connection between our brief mortal lives and eternity. Yew energy, with its multi-million years of consciousness, teaches us to be fully present in the Here and Now and to appreciate each moment as a unique gift. This is the real Gateway to Renewal."

Tom   *To Julie* What? What did you say?

Kevin   She didn't say anything.

Julie *With a small smile.* You see, that's why I have to go to class Tom!

Tom, Julie and Kevin form a kind of circle around the tree, with books in hand, talking, chatting, looking at things in the books, comparing, and using some signing with Tom. At a distance, May is watching, with April in carriage.

The end

www.ingramcontent.com/pod-product-compliance
Lightning Source LLC
Chambersburg PA
CBHW022033090426
42741CB00007B/1051